I0471438

Sell It Online 2

How to Make Money with Your Own Website, Blog, Kindle Book, or by Coaching &Training

Copyright © 2013 by Nick Vulich

Thank you for purchasing this book. **Sell It Online 2** is an attempt to bring you easy to implement solutions for starting your online business. While no book can guarantee you success, the author and publisher have made every attempt to bring you the latest information that has been found to work for other online sellers. As with anything else in life results can vary, based on the time you invest and your approach to implementing the various ideas and strategies given.

If you find the contents helpful, please consider taking a few moments to leave a review on Amazon.

Your comments will help other readers decide if this book may be useful to them as they search for more information about how to sell online. They will also help me to catch errors or omissions in this book, and to correct them as quickly as possible.

Contact me at: nick@digitalhistoryproject.com.

If you really like what you read, and are feeling a little extra love, help me get the message out there. Tweet and share this book with all of your friends on Facebook. If you know someone who is dreaming about starting a career in online sales, gift them a copy or two.

Finally, I want to take a moment to let you know, I don't make any money from any of the links in this book. I think affiliate links are the curse of eBooks, and shy away from using them.

Table of Contents

There are a lot of books out there that tell people how to make money online. I'm sure you've probably seen a few of them –

- 61 Ways to Make Money Online
- 99 Ways to Make Money Online
- 101 Ways to Make Money at Home Working in your Pajamas

The problem with these kinds of books is: They give you a laundry list of ideas on how you might make money, but they don't really give you the information you need to do it.

It's like buying a hamburger, minus the meat. You're missing the best part of the sandwich.

When I read through these works, what pops into my mind, is the teacher talking on the old Charlie Brown cartoons, "blah, blah – blah, blah – blah, blah."

When you're done reading the book, you're all psyched up, but you're not really sure how to get started. Most of these books are link heavy, meaning they send you off to other sites to get the information you need. The problem is, a lot of the sites they send you to are just as light on information as the book you just read, or they want you to ante up twenty bucks or fifty bucks to teach you what to do.

So what happens?

You're money making project gets put on the back burner, and eventually fizzles out.

I'm sorry to be the one to tell you, but that's the way it works. For most of you reading this book, it's not the first **Make Money Online** book you've read. Most people read five to seven books on the subject. It's a lot like that old potato chip jingle, except "no one can read just one."

What I've chosen to do in this book is narrow the list down to just four money making ideas. My thought is with just four, it will present enough ideas, where everyone will find at least one idea they can work with, yet it will allow me the opportunity to fully develop the idea for you.

I promise not to load you down with hundreds of links, and I won't send you to any affiliate sites. Some less shameless authors fill their books with affiliate links, where they make a fat juicy commission check for every purchase you make.

I'm going to give you everything you need to get started. You can read this book this morning, and get started this evening, with no other information products to buy - ever.

Introduction

My previous book **Sell It Online** covered several ways to make money online: Selling on eBay, Amazon, Fiverr, and Etsy.

This book offers four other approaches where you're not so much selling, as sharing the knowledge you have. I have personally used each of these methods. They have worked well for me and other people that I know. They can work for you, as well, if you follow the directions, and give them a chance.

To make the cut for this book, each of the methods given had to meet the following criteria.

1) *You need to be able to get started for under $100.*

My thought is, most people who want to start an online business, don't want to put a lot of money into it. If you make the barrier too high, people are going to be afraid to take the leap. One hundred bucks seems like a hurdle most people will be able to make.

2) *It's got to be so easy to get started your grandmother could do it.*

Face it, I can give you step-by-step instructions on how to plant a tree that grows one hundred dollar bills, but you're not going to do it if the instructions are overly complicated.

3) *It has to put money in your pocket within 90 days*.

No one wants to wait forever to see their business payoff. Every one of the businesses, I'm going to share with you has the potential to put some jingle in your pocket within 90 days. Several of them can bring you cash in the first week, or two.

Kindle Book Marketing

I liken Kindle to the new internet gold rush. All of the gurus out there are sharing stories about five or six lucky authors who have managed to make hundreds of thousands of dollars from their Kindle books.

That much is true. A few people have made some really big bucks promoting their Kindle books. Another truth is, most people who publish a Kindle book, end up watching it wither and die in no time at all. The lucky ones sell one hundred copies a year; the not so lucky ones sell three or four copies. But, then they run out of mothers, grandmothers, and best friends to keep their sales going.

With that said, there is a middle group of Kindle authors, selling five hundred to two thousand copies of their books every month. Many of them are pulling down a cool $1000 to $5000 per month in royalties.

In this section we will explore the latter group of Kindle authors, and lay out their secrets for success.

Local employment website or local portal

This is a specialized market not many people are aware of. It is easy to break into. In as little as six months you can be pulling down $1000 or more in monthly income.

Don't know anything about HTML or website publishing, not a problem. I will show you everything you need to succeed in this business.

Online training courses and coaching

Do people always ask you for advice on how to do something? Are you the go to person at your company, or in a group? Do you enjoy helping people learn new tasks?

If so, creating online courses and training materials might be the perfect opportunity for you.

Blogging

Blogging is a great way to share your passions with the world, while being able to make a little money, too.

I'm not going to lie to you.

Most people don't make a whole lot of money blogging. Often times they make enough to cover their expenses, and a few bucks to take the family out to dinner now and then. Other bloggers have broken loose and made six and seven figure incomes blogging.

It can happen. I'm just saying don't bet all your chips on it.

Running a successful blog takes a lot of work; a lot of writing; and even more persistence in employing every traffic building tactic you can find.

I've been writing Kindle books for almost a year now, and it really is one of the best ways to make money online.

It's also a lot of work.

One book normally isn't going to make you a whole lot of money. The real magic starts happening as you grow your backlist, and have eight to ten books in print.

So how do you get started?

1) First off you need a great idea.

2) You need to produce a well written book.

3) You need to publish your book.

4) Just because you published a book doesn't mean anybody's going to read it. You need to get the word out, and help people find your book.

5) The Kindle world has very few one book wonders. If you want to make money writing, the best advice I can give you, is as soon as you're done writing a book, get started writing your next book.

Successful book ideas

I don't know about you, but every time I start thinking about writing a new book, my knees get to shaking, and I start biting my fingernails.

Finding a book topic is a lot like shopping for a new car. You really have to work to find the right one. For me, I need to try it on, and make sure that it's going to be a good fit for me. After all, I'm going to be spending from one week to three months working on it.

What I normally do is start by brainstorming topics. After I get a list of twenty or thirty possible ideas, I start to narrow it down a bit. When I've got my list down to three or four ideas, I start exploring them in more detail.

The first thing I do is to start typing my idea into the Amazon search bar. What I'm looking for is a quick overview of what's out there. I want to know how many books have been written on my topic, how well they are selling, and how other authors approached the subject.

The really great thing about doing your initial research on Amazon is you are looking at current book titles. When you come across one that sounds interesting, take a look at the description. If it looks like it has possibilities, take a peek inside. Amazon lets you read the first ten percent of most books, so you can check out the table of contents, the writing style, and some of the information they are offering.

Don't stop there. You should also take a look at the reader reviews. Most of them are only a line or two. They don't tell you much, except whether they liked the book or not. Some of the longer reviews will tell you why they liked the book, or what they hated about it. The really good reviews tell you what they wish would have been included in the book.

This is all gold. It will help you shape your book. Make sure you have your notebook out and are taking copious notes during your research.

One other great piece of information you can pick up on Amazon is how well books on your topic are selling. Midway down the book description page you're going to come across a section titled "Product Details." At the very bottom of that section it tells you the "Amazon Best Seller Ranking." If the book is ranked in a category, it will show you the ranking, and the category it is ranked in.

It also shows you the book's ranking in the paid Kindle Store. The lower the number, the better the book is selling. Most authors look for several books in a category to be ranked at 20,000, or lower. This means the book is selling four to six copies a day, which gives you a shot at making some decent money. A ranking of 50,000 means the book is probably selling one to two books a day. A ranking of 100,000 means the book is selling about one or two copies a week. A ranking above 500,000 means the book is selling one copy a month.

Unless you've got a really great message, or some startling new discovery, you probably want to table an idea, if there aren't at least one or two books in the category that rank under 20,000.

You need to produce a well written book

You don't have to be another Stephen King or Amanda Hocking, but you do need to know how to turn a phrase.

If you're writing nonfiction people will be more forgiving of grammatical errors, as long as you give them the information you promised them. If you're writing a novel, people expect to be entertained, and you had better be at the top of your game if you want to make big sales.

Keep in mind, no book is going to be perfect, especially on the first go around. Every book should go through several rounds of proof reading for grammatical errors and typos.

One of the fastest ways to get your book torn apart in the Kindle market is to publish a poorly written book, loaded with typos. It's going to put you on the fast track to bad reviews.

Not only will it tank this book, but probably your next book offering, too.

If you're not up to the task of editing your own book, ask a friend who is good with English. Another option is to hire a proof reader or copy editor on Fiverr, or another freelancing site.

Get your manuscript ready for publication

Publishing your book on Kindle is relatively easy.

I've read a lot of complicated descriptions on how to properly format your manuscript in HTML or using this or that eBook program. The truth is – you can do it just as well in MS Word.

Here are a few tips for taming your manuscript using Word.

1) Set your page margins to six inches times nine inches.

2) Don't paste your pictures into the text. Use Word's insert picture function. This will ensure your pictures are displayed properly.

3) Insert a page break after each section. This will give your readers a better reading experience by being able to start each new section on a fresh page.

4) Stick with the basic fonts. Use Arial, Calibri, or Times Roman in either 11 or 12 point size type.

5) Don't try to format your eBook like you would a print book. People are going to read your eBook on all sorts

of different reading devices – Kindle, PC, Phone, and Tablets.

Another thing to remember is readers have the ability to change the font and typestyle for most books. Make sure your basic layout is good, and everything else will be fine.

6) Add a clickable table of contents to your book. This is easier than it sounds, and will make your book appear more professional.

To get started: Go through your manuscript and highlight the chapter titles. After you highlight each chapter title, click on *Heading 1* in the *Home* section of the toolbar. Do this for each chapter.

Next, highlight all of your sub-headings, and select Heading style 2. This will differentiate them from the chapter titles when they appear in your table of contents.

The last step is to add your table of contents. To do this, go to a blank page where you want to insert your table of contents. Click on the *References* tab in the upper toolbar. At the far left, you will see *Table of Contents*. Click on it. Select *Insert Table of Contents*. A little further down you're going to see a checkmark where it says *Show Page Numbers*. Click on the box with the checkmark to remove it. Click OK at the bottom of the page.

One last step and you're done.

Type the words "Table of Contents" at the top of the page. Highlight it, and select *Insert Bookmark*. Type "toc" where it asks you to insert the *bookmark name*. This tells Kindle this is your table of contents, and will make it available to readers as a menu option.

Publish your book

There are a lot of options available to authors who want to self-publish their book. Among the more popular sites are Kindle, Barnes & Noble, Smash Words, Kobo, and iTunes.

My recommendation is to start with Kindle. Branch out to other sites after you've got some experience under your belt.

The reason I recommend Kindle is they currently control over 65 percent of the eBook market. You're a writer. You might as well go where the readers are. Right?

To get started on Kindle click on the following link: https://kdp.amazon.com/self-publishing/signin

Follow the directions to sign up for a Kindle Direct Publishing account.

When you're ready to publish your book, select the option to *Add a New Title*.

The first thing you're asked is to *Enroll this book in KDP Select*. My suggestion is to check this box. KDP is an amazing way to promote your book on Amazon. What happens is: Every ninety days you are enrolled in KDP, Amazon helps you build your audience by allowing you to give away free downloads of your book for five days.

Description

When you get to description, stop and think for a moment. This is the information readers are going to use to determine whether they want to buy your book or not.

Some authors write very short descriptions. That's a waste of valuable real estate. Your description needs to tell people what your book is about. It should be informative, enticing, and written in a style similar to the way your book is written.

I like to start off by asking a question, and then go into more detail. Sometimes authors begin with a shocking fact or startling statistic. Other publishers lead into their descriptions by showing portions of the reviews they've received.

The thing to remember is: There's no set way you have to write your description. Make it fit you, and your book. If your book is really short, and very little of it appears in the preview, you may want to include an excerpt in your description.

Target your book

You're going to enter two key components for your book's success here.

The first thing you're asked to do is to select two categories for your book. When selecting categories, keep in mind the category your book lands in can make or break it.

Amazon has millions of titles. When most people search for a book to read, they browse categories. In order for your book to sell, it needs to be found, and to be found, it's crucial for your book to be ranked among the top 100 books in its category. Many people only look at the top 20 books in a category before they click away.

So the category you choose is going to play a big role in determining the success of your book.

Some authors suggest you pick easy categories starting out to ensure your book will rank high. They put their books in marginal categories that aren't the best fit for their title. I've always gone for the category I want to rank in. If my book is a Presidential biography, that's the category I choose. If my book is about selling on eBay, I choose the ecommerce category in business and computers.

If you're in doubt, check what categories your closest competitors are listed in and go with those. After your book has been on the site awhile, Amazon will eventually slot your book into the categories they think it will sell best in.

You're also asked to add keywords people will search for your book on.

The keywords you choose are crucial to your books success. The keywords I chose for this book are: online marketing, Stacie Davidson, online consulting and training, coaching business, kindle book writing and marketing, local website publishing, blog marketing, Steve Scott.

Notice, none of them are single words. Think about how you search for a book. You might start with eBay, then move out to eBay Profits, or online auction sales. This book includes several methods of conducting an online business. Other people search by author, so I've tagged a couple popular books and authors in my category.

As the book starts to sell, I will probably keep refining my list of keywords, until I get down to seven I feel will really get the job done.

Upload book cover and book file

Best advice you will ever get. No matter how good you think you are, never, ever, design your own book cover.

Here's a review one of my books received with a self-designed cover: "Got this during a free promo. No way

I would have paid money for it with this cheesy cover, but it's actually a decent book."

Despite what people say: That you can't judge a book by its cover, everybody does.

Think about the last time you bought a book. One of two things caught your eye: Either the title or the cover. Maybe, a little bit of both.

Designing a great cover doesn't need to be expensive. Sure you can commission someone to create custom artwork, and get the most unique design out there. That can easily cost you $500, $1000, or more. I take a slightly different tack, and hire several different designers on Fiverr to create a cover for me. This gives me a number of covers to choose from. I put the best one on Kindle.

This also gives me a fall back strategy. If sales aren't what I expect, I can switch out covers and see if it helps my sales.

I'm writing this in mid-June. My eBay book sales have been sluggish to say the least. One day I noticed several of the regular sellers in my category had switched out their covers and were making some headway on the charts. I gave it a shot, too, and sure enough it gave a number of my titles a temporary boost in sales.

Preview your book

At the bottom of the first page you have the opportunity to preview your book as it would look on Kindle, and Kindle for PC.

Do it. Do it more than once.

One of the things I always do is download a copy of my book to my Kindle Fire every few days as I'm writing it. That way I can read it in the format my readers are going to see it in.

This does two things:

1) It forces me to read the book the way most of my readers will.

2) It alerts me to any formatting errors so I can get them corrected before publication.

Whatever you do, don't publish your book with formatting errors. Readers will blast you with terrible reviews and tank your book.

Verify rights and set price

At the top of the second page, you are asked to verify your publishing rights. Normally, if you are the author of the work, you just click worldwide, and let her rip. If there is some reason why you can only publish your book in certain areas, select those areas, and you're ready to roll.

Pricing is a sensitive area for most authors. We all want to get as much money as we can for our books, but you have to balance that with what readers are willing to pay.

Amazon gives you some guidance based upon the royalties they pay.

- Books priced between 99 cents and $2.98 pay the author a 35 percent royalty.
- Books priced between $2.99 and $9.99 pay the author a 70 percent royalty.
- Books priced over $9.99, from $10.00 to $200.00 (the maximum amount you can charge on Kindle) pay a 35 percent royalty.

This tells us Amazon feels the sweet spot for Kindle books is between $2.99 and $9.99. We know this because this is where they pay authors the highest royalties.

From my personal experience books priced at $2.99 sell really well; at $3.99 you're going to encounter some resistance; depending upon how long your book is, and what the competition is charging, your book may still sell ok at $4.99 and $5.99. Anything over $5.99 and you're going to hit some serious resistance, unless you are a celebrity, or a big name author.

You will also come across a lot of authors pushing their books for 99 cents. That creates a very steep slope to climb if you intend to make any money.

A 99 cent book pays 35 percent royalties. You make 35 cents for each copy sold. To make ten bucks, you need to sell thirty books, whereas at $2.99, you only need to sell five books to make that same ten bucks.

That's not to say 99 cents is a bad pricing strategy. I use it when my sales are weak. Last month one of my titles ran out of steam. I priced it at 99 cents for three weeks to try and pick up some momentum. It sold 100 copies at 99 cents, and since I returned the price to $2.99 this month, it is on course to sell 60 copies.

After you've entered your price, check the box at the bottom where it asks you to confirm rights, and then click publish.

In less than twelve hours you will be a published writer.

I've published my book, now what?

That's a good question.

The very first thing you want to do is download a copy and read it over good. Look for formatting issues, typos, and grammatical errors. This is your last chance to change things before readers get a peek at it.

If you're happy with everything, the next step is to schedule your free promo days. Everybody has a different strategy on this. My thought is five days works the best for new authors. It gives you time to build momentum. Normally your first few days are going to be slow, but as time moves on people will start downloading more copies.

Getting Reviews

Another magical thing begins to happen around day three of your free giveaway; you start getting reviews. I read somewhere you average one review for every thousand copies downloaded or sold. That means, if you get 5,000 free downloads you can figure you will get five reviews. Sometimes you get more. Sometimes you can have a great giveaway and not get any reviews. Don't sweat it, it happens.

I was really worried with my first few books. Reviews were scarce, and everybody said, "You can't sell books without reviews." I finally asked some friends to review my book. Some of them did, some didn't, but most of those reviews weren't very helpful. Friends tend to write one or two line reviews that go something like this, "A great read. I really liked it."

The thing is readers like reviews to have a little meat to them. They want to know why the reviewer liked the book, or why they didn't like it. They want to know why the reviewer found your book useful or entertaining.

Don't worry. Those reviews will come. Twenty books, and nearly a year later, I now have over 100 reviews. A lot of them are really great four and five star reviews, a few of them are one and two star reviews. Good reviews happen, so do bad reviews. All of them will help sell your books.

Kindle Book Marketing 101

There's a lot of advice out there about how to market your book. I'm not a big believer in any of it.

I've sold thousands of books in the last year without doing anything other than optimizing my Amazon profile. So what I'm going to do is show you how to maximize your profile on Amazon, then I will refer you to a few books on advanced marketing techniques for book authors.

Book Description

Earlier we talked about your book description, when we discussed how to list your book on Kindle.

What you need to understand is your book description is a work in progress. You want to keep tweaking it. Test different versions, until you get the best description you can.

Never be satisfied until you get the sales you want. Try writing a description of your book; introduce your characters; offer a book summary; lead with complimentary reviews; as you become better-known, talk more about yourself.

The thing is: You never know what's going to attract people's attention until you give it a shot.

Amazon Author Central

Amazon created Author Central as an area for writer's to showcase information about themselves and their works.

One thing we know: If people like your work, they're going to want to know more about you; what you look like; how you got started writing; where you live; and what other books you've published.

To claim your Author Central page, visit the following link:

https://authorcentral.amazon.com/gp/home?ie=UTF 8&pn=irid37437482

Upload an author biography to introduce yourself. Add a picture so readers can have a look at your bright and smiling face. Author Central also gives you a place to collect all of your books in one place so readers can browse through them. Each time you publish a new book, be sure to click on Add Book, to add you latest tile to your list of books.

Another interesting option Amazon offers is the ability to link your blog and Twitter account to your Author Central Account. When you do this your most recent tweet shows up, along with highlights from your three most recent blog posts. Talk about a great way to engage your readers, and get them to follow you.

You also have a spot to upload book trailers or promotional videos. If you're photogenic, or good with video, you could create a whole series of videos to allow readers to learn more about you and your books.

A lot of people link their books to Facebook or their author website, but a link to Author Central might pay off better in the long run. Not only does it introduce readers to you, it gives you a great opportunity to sell more of your books.

Final Thoughts

Writing an eBook is a great way to make some extra money.

Don't let the hype fool you. One book isn't going to make you rich. Over time, if it is well written, and on a popular topic, it can bring you several hundred dollars per month in royalties.

The real magic starts when you have a backlist of ten to twenty books in a related field. When this happens people will read one of your books, and if they like it, chances are they will pick up one or two more. Some of them may even read all of your books.

My best advice is, if you want to make money writing, look at each book as a stepping stone to a larger audience and increased sales.

Finally, most of the information I have shared with you has focused on optimizing your Amazon profile to increase book sales. Many authors insist a strong author platform is your best marketing tool.

Their thought is you need an author website, a blog, and at the minimum, a Facebook and Twitter account.

For more information on building an author platform you can check out the following books:

. *Building Your Fanbase: A From Scratch Guide for Indie Authors*, by Duolit and Shannon O'Neil.

. *Blog It! The Author's Guide to Building a Successful Online Brand*, by Molly Greene.

. *Book Marketing Basics: How to Use Facebook, Twitter, Blogging, and Email Marketing to Connect With Readers*, by Duolit.

. *Giving the Bird: The Indie Author's Guide to Twitter*, by Benjamin Wallace.

. *Twitter For Authors: Social Media Book Marketing Strategies for Shy Authors*, by Beth Barany.

. *The Social Media Superstar Handbook*, by Lisa Pietsch.

Running a blog can be the most fun you ever have while working, but make no mistake about it - It's a lot of hard work.

Here are some of the things it takes to be a successful blogger:

1) **A Great Topic**. The success of your blog is ultimately going to come down to the topic you pick. The more people that are interested in it, the larger your potential audience will be.

2) **Interesting Content**. There are millions of different blogs out there. People are only going to read yours if you can supply a steady stream of interesting content.

3) **Basic Writing Skills**. You don't have to be another Hemingway or Faulkner, but you do need to know the basics of how to string a few sentences together. You should also know the ins and outs of your word processor, including how to use spellcheck and how to clean up those squiggly green lines the grammar checker shows.

4) **Ability to consistently post content**. To be a successful blogger you need to consistently create and post new content. Too many blogs are unsuccessful, and fade away and die, because the owner fails to provide new content.

5) **Unique content**. Not only do you have to provide well written, interesting content; it also needs to be unique. If you want to build an audience you have to provide unique new content before others do.

6) **Video, audio, photo skills**. People expect more than words. You need to be able to create a variety of content, including videos, photos, and audio recordings.

7) **Basic SEO Skills**. You need to be able to identify keywords, and know how to write your blog posts and titles so they will be optimized for Search Engine Optimization. You need to organize your content so it will be easy for search engines to find, and identify your content.

8) **Monetization skills**. At some point, you're going to want your blog to make money. To do that, you need to find different ways to monetize it, either through selling ads on your site, or by selling content such as eBooks or other information products.

9) **Stick-to-it-iveness**. What do I mean by this? You need to stick with it, even when you're sure no one is looking at your content. You need to keep posting great content, even when it means missing a golf game, a movie, or special time with your family.

Some blogs take right off. But, most often, it will take some time for your blog to gain momentum and pick up followers.

That's why it's so important to choose a popular topic you are also passionate about. You're going to be spending a lot of time with it, make sure you enjoy it.

Choosing your blog topic

More than anything else, the topic you choose to blog about is going to determine your success.

In my experience these are the most popular topics people tune into:

1) Love

2) Money

3) Celebrity gossip

4) Mom info

5) Look good

6) Feel good

7) Hobbies

8) Weight loss

Choosing any one of these topics will help you to draw traffic right out of the box.

But, to really become successful, you need to focus on just one small section of a topic, not the entire topic.

Here's what I mean. There are probably a million blogs about how to make money online. If you choose to blog about making money online, your message is going to get lost in the clutter.

If you narrow your blog topic down, and instead concentrate on How to make money selling textbooks on Amazon, your audience is going to be much smaller. It's also going to be more focused. Everyone who visits your site is going to be interested in that topic. As long as you continue providing relevant content they will keep returning to your blog.

Weight loss is another one of those subjects everybody and their brother has a blog or a website on. That doesn't mean you can't launch a successful blog about weight loss, it means you need to develop your own niche. Focus on a theme: Weight Loss for Men over Fifty, Tone Your Thighs and Firm Your Buttocks, How to Lose Weight after Pregnancy.

The narrower your niche, the easier it will be to provide quality relevant content to your audience.

Setting up your blog

There are a lot of great blogging platforms available: Blogger, Word Press, Tumblr, Typepad. Any of them will work for your new blog.

The two most popular options are Blogger and Word Press. They offer more flexibility and control over your blog.

Personally, I prefer Blogger. It's easy to use. It offers a good variety of themes and layouts, and it's easy to monetize (they have a built in option to add Google AdSense). You have the option of assigning a custom URL to your blog, which gives it a more professional look and feel.

Other people swear by Word Press. It offers more features than Blogger; is served up on an independent platform, so you have total control over your blog; has thousands of pre-made themes you can download and apply to your blog; and it allows you to use a custom URL.

The choice ultimately comes down to which you prefer. Either one will do a great job for you.

What kind of content will you provide?

Content is king on your blog.

You need to consistently provide great content that educates, informs, and entertains your audience. If your content is bad, it doesn't matter how many readers you draw to your blog, they won't bookmark your site and return for another serving.

With that said, what kind of content should you provide?

Here is a short list of the types of posts you should try to provide:

1) **Lists**. People go goo-goo ga-ga over lists. These are some of the most popular blog posts you can write. It can be as simple as a list of the top ten ways to save money on Wi-Fi, or Twenty-five ways to lose stubborn belly fat.

There's something about a list that makes people want to take a peek and see what they're missing. Hint: Include a number in your title and readership will triple. I don't know what it is, but including a number in your title reels people in.

2) **Short informational posts**. These are some of the easiest posts you will write. They should be somewhere between 300 to 500 words and focused on a single topic. Make it informative, but light and easy to read.

You should write three or four of these posts every month. They're a quick easy way for you to connect with your audience.

3) **Wrap up or overview post**. In a wrap up post you pick a topic, and curate content on it. If I was publishing a celebrity blog, I might write a post about celebrity baby bumps. I could do a review piece, highlighting content that has been hosted on other blogs or news magazines in the past week, month, or whatever period I am looking at.

This post is going to take a little longer to put together because you need to gather links, and then write a short article that ties them all together. This type of post is a great way to add video to your blog by embedding You-Tube videos.

Depending upon your subject you can do one of these posts every week, every two weeks, or every month. It's the type of post people will keep coming back for if you can provide them with good useful links.

4) **Tell a story**. Everybody loves to hear a good story. At least once a month you should share a story with your audience. It doesn't have to be long, 250 to 500 words is fine. It can be about something that happened to you, about a historical event, or something happening in the news. Be sure to keep it light and entertaining.

5) **Informational post**. These are the pillar of your blog. They offer an in depth look at one particular aspect of your topic. These posts can run anywhere between 1500 to 3500 words depending upon the subject.

For these posts to be effective, they need to contain a lot of unique, useful information. They should contain links to outside sources, videos, other people's blogs.

The easiest way to discover a relevant topic is to Google "hot topics in *****." The search results should return things your audience is interested in right now. Pick one, and give your audience the answers they need to form an opinion.

6) **Interview someone in your field**. One of the easiest ways to become an authority figure is to be seen in the company of people who already have the authority you want. Interviewing a celebrity or authority figure is a great way to piggy back off of their fame.

Getting started is easier than you think. If you want to interview another blogger, check out their contact page and drop them an email. Keep it short and to the point. Give them a link to your blog, and explain what you want to do.

You can do the same thing with the author of a book concerning your blog topic. Contact the author, and let them know you are looking at reviewing their book, and you would like to include a sidebar about them. Most authors will be glad to answer a few questions, and even supply a current photo you can publish with the interview. Make it a win – win for both of you.

Whenever I've been interviewed or conducted an interview, we normally swap questions and answers by email, and follow up with a short phone call to follow up on any questions that might come up.

7) **How to post**. People love how to posts. They can be as short as one hundred words, or as long as several thousand words depending upon what you are trying to explain.

How to posts offer a great opportunity to add video, especially if it's a hand's on project. Let me give you an example: My wife broke the "H" key on her computer. She purchased the repair kit online for $7.00, but didn't know how to install it. Along comes You-Tube to the rescue with a detailed video showing how to replace a computer key.

You can create your own videos, or you can find a series of videos on You-Tube and present links to them to help solve your reader's problems.

Posting schedule

Search engines love websites that consistently add new and unique content. The more often you add content, the more often they will send their spiders out to search for it.

Starting out as a new blogger your first goal will be to post ten or fifteen articles as quickly as possible. Content is the most important thing at this point. You want to have enough articles on your blog to convince your audience you can deliver the info they want.

Once you've posted your initial articles you should develop a regular blogging schedule.

One or two posts a week is probably fine starting out, especially if you are delivering great content. Shake them up a bit. Offer some informational posts, some short posts, a how to, an interview, and a wrap up. People come in different flavors, and you can never be sure which type of post they will find more enjoyable.

Statistical tracking

Blogging is sort of like taking a trip.

When we were kids we always watched the odometer to figure out how far we traveled on a vacation. A statistical tracker does the same thing for your blog; it lets you see how much traffic your blog receives. What I like about blogger is it has a blog stats feature built into the control panel. I can tell at a glance what my top blog posts were for the day, week, or all time; where the traffic came from; what operating system they used; and the keywords they searched on to bring them there.

For more detailed information you can install Google Analytics on your blog. It's easy to use. You just need to sign up for the service (It's free), and copy the tracking code into each of your posts. Google Analytics gives you awesome details about your website visitors, down to which pages they entered and exited your blog from, and how long they spent viewing each post.

My recommendation is to spend an hour every week or two reviewing your stats. It will give you some great insight into your visitors, and where they are spending their time on your blog. The answer might be totally different than what you expect. You'll never know until you check.

Monetizing your blog

You have many choices when it comes to monetizing your blog.

The most popular choice is Google AdSense. AdSense lets you place display and text ads in strategic spots on your blog. Each time one of your readers clicks on an ad Google pays you a percentage of the revenue they earned on it.

Over time Google gets really good at matching ads to your website so more people click on them. The bad part is you aren't going to make a lot of money from AdSense until you start to have some good traffic numbers. My Q C Jobs website averages 5,000 to 6,000 visitors per month. AdSense revenue averages around $150 to $200 per month.

Depending on your content you can find a number of affiliate programs that might fit in. Adult Friend Finder has a great affiliate program if you have a dating site. If your blog focuses on a profession or technical area, you might want to look at job links from Indeed and Simply Hired.

Some of the bigger affiliate sites you should investigate are Commission Junction and Link Share. They offer programs from some of America's largest businesses. Be aware most of the advertisers reserve the right to accept or reject your website. If your content or visitor count doesn't mesh with their minimum requirements, you won't be accepted. Keep trying and eventually you should be able to find a number of offers that will be attractive to your audience.

eBay has one of the best affiliate program, if you can get accepted. I've tried with several different sites, and have been rejected for all of them. Despite that I still have eBay ads on my site it's just that they're displayed there through Google AdSense.

Amazon Affiliates is another program used by a lot of bloggers. With Amazon you can use their widgets to build an entire store full of products targeted to your niche, or you can select individual items. The cool thing here is if you have a big enough audience you could review a book or movie and link to it with your Amazon Affiliate account. Each time one of your readers purchases it, you would receive a cut of the profits.

Finally, you can sell individual ad spots on your blog. Some blogs have large banner ads; others offer smaller ads they label as sponsors. Either way offers you the opportunity to pick up a few extra bucks.

Final wrap up

Blogging is a fun way to reach out to like-minded people, and have the opportunity to make some extra money at the same time. Just remember, it's not a sure thing, and it's not a get rich quick scheme. You need to put in the time, and build an audience.

Content is king. If you plan on being a successful blogger you need to provide a lot of unique entertaining content.

Local employment website

I've been running an employment website for several years now. It's a great source for extra income.

Most job seekers visit the big four job boards:

1) Monster

2) CareerBuilder

3) Simply Hired

4) Indeed

Major metropolitan areas generally have one or two other "local" sites. These are most often sponsored by the local media, such as newspapers, radio and TV stations.

If you take a look at any of them, they have the same generic look. They feature ten to twenty job postings on each page. Everything else is covered with display ads. They use so much script it takes the pages forever to load.

This gives you the opportunity to stand out and do something totally unique. Rather than just feature job postings, you can custom tailor a site for the area you live in.

One such site is qcjobsforyou.com, located in the Iowa / Illinois Quad Cities.

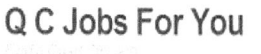

Q C Jobs For You has a unique look.

It's laid out as a magazine style website, and contains articles about job hunting strategies, resumes, cover letters, interviewing, and information on the local economy. Some of the local information includes info on the area's largest employers, local employment training programs, and career placement contacts.

The site is broken into sections for easy reference by job seekers looking for specific information. There is also a job search store, featuring books relevant to job seekers. The book store is powered by Amazon Associates and is an extra source of income for the job board.

A career site gives you a real opportunity to form a relationship within your community. Done properly, it can make you a job search or career coach expert in your area.

It's also more hands on than other opportunities discussed in this guide. To really make it work, you need to be out in your community, talking to local businesses, forming relationships, sniffing out stories, and writing articles for your site.

How do you get started?

The first question most people ask is: Where am I going to find the jobs to list?

The good news is: Two of the big four sites, Simply Hired and Indeed have affiliate programs that will give you an unending supply of jobs for your job board. They also pay you a juicy commission whenever job seekers click on sponsored ads.

To get started you need to sign up for their affiliate programs.

. **Indeed**

https://ads.indeed.com/jobroll/

. **Simply Hired**

http://www.jobamatic.com/jbb-static/home

To become an affiliate you need to fill out the online forms. Once you are accepted into the program you will be given access to the codes needed to generate your job boards and links.

I know, codes and links sound complicated, but they make them really easy to use. If you can cut and paste with your word processor you have all the high tech skills you need to build a job board.

Using the Indeed Job board

My personal preference is Indeed. They're easy to use; their payout threshold is $100.00; so you get paid sooner. I've consistently received bigger commission checks from them.

With that said, I like the look and feel of the Simply Hired job board better. My recommendation is to look them over, and decide which one you prefer. If you're unsure, switch back and forth between them, and see which one brings you better results.

Setting up your Indeed job board is a breeze. When you open up the Indeed dashboard, click on the Instant Job Site tab.

Most of the information is self-explanatory. *Show jobs* from the web lets Indeed post jobs from their website on your job board. *Allow visitors to post jobs*, enables a screen for employers to post jobs at the fee you set. If you want to *pre-approve job posting* before they are put up, you have the ability to do that by checking the appropriate box.

Indeed gives you the option to choose what type of jobs you would like your board to show when job seekers click into your job board. I recommend leaving this section blank. When you leave it blank, it shows a selection of jobs from all categories. Next pick the default area, i.e. the city or state you are serving.

Click update, and you will be taken to the next page with the HTML code for your site.

Here is what the job board code looks like:

```
<script type="text/javascript">
var indeed_publisher_id = '8234710805684';
</script>
<script type="text/javascript"
src="http://www.indeed.com/p/jobsite.js"></script>
<noscript><a
href="http://www.indeed.com/p/?pid=8234710805684">Jo
b Search</a></noscript>
```

It creates your job board, and has your publisher id embedded in it so Indeed can pay you every time someone clicks on a sponsored ad.

Another feature you will want to take advantage of is listed under the Create Job Roll tab. This allows you to make customized job search boxes to sprinkle throughout your site. More clicks mean more money.

Using the Simply Hired job board

Setting up a Simply Hired job board is similar to what we did with Indeed.

The first thing you are asked to do is name your job board. After that you enter an email address for customer support. The sidebar promotion box allows you to control how many promotional links Simply Hired shows on your website. Experiment, and see what you like best. Finally, you set a price for new job postings, and set how long each ad will run. Normal posting length is either 14, or 30 days.

Simply Hired has several other features, not included on Indeed that will help you make more money.

The Job search widget is similar to Indeed's job roll, and allows you to place targeted job search boxes on your website.

Another tool offered by Simply Hired is their banners and links section. It helps you promote your job ads.

One other nifty tool Simply Hired offers is their Job Packages tool. What this does is give you the opportunity to discount job postings when buyers purchase multiple listings.

Some of the packages you can offer are three listings for the price of two, or unlimited job postings for thirty days.

Finding a place to host your job board

We've created the code to build your job board, now you need a place to put it.

The two web hosting solutions I've had good luck with are <u>Blogger</u> and <u>Page Farm</u>.

Blogger is a blogging platform hosted by Google. It is incredibly easy to use. For the most part you just type in your information, insert a picture, press post, and you're good to go. Another great benefit of using Blogger is: It's FREE!

Page Farm is a little more complicated to use, but it will give your site a great magazine style look similar to that of Q C Jobs For You. Page Farm also gives you more control over formatting than blogger. But, those extra features are going to cost you $29.00 a month.

What you may want to do is experiment with setting up a site on Blogger to see what you think. Then take advantage of Page Farm's thirty day free trial to see what you can cook up there. At the end of the thirty day trial, choose the option you like best.

Registering your domain name

After you decide which site to host your job board on, you need to register your domain name.

The domain name stakes out your claim on the internet. It makes it possible for search engines to find you.

After you've picked a name for your website, visit Go Daddy. They have a tool to check your domain name to make sure it is available. If Go Daddy shows the name you want is unavailable you have two choices. You can choose a different name, or a different extension. Dot com is the most common type of domain, but if you found a name you really like, chances are it will be available with a different extension such as .info, .org, or .biz.

Once you've selected the perfect domain, and ensured it is available, you need to register it. Again Blogger makes it the easiest to register a domain name, because they have it available as an option in their dashboard.

If you host your site with Page Farm or another provider, you will need to purchase a domain name from Go Daddy or another domain registrar, and then link it back to your website. It's a little more work, but the guys at Page Farm helped me through it on my first go around.

Tips for setting up your site with Blogger

If you're using Blogger, the dashboard will walk you through setting up your site.

My suggestion is to go with a basic style layout. Blogger offers some fancier options, but the classic style will give you more choices as far as getting the right look to monetize your blog.

Your best bet is to design a simple logo for your blog header. If you need help designing your header, visit Fiverr.

Adjust the right sidebar so you will have 350 pixels for it. This will give you room to place a standard 250 x 300 banner ad (we will talk more about this later).

Use the page option to set up website pages. You will need to set up at least five.

1) **Search Jobs**. This one will host your job board.

2) **Contact Info**. Tell viewers how to get in touch with you.

3) **About us**. This is where you're going to share a little information about your website, and a short bio about yourself.

4) **Job Search Store**. You can use Amazon Affiliates to add a book store here for extra profits.

5) **Featured Jobs**. If you want to upsell advertisers, you can set up a featured jobs page.

This will get your basic site up and running.

Tips for setting up your site with Page Farm

Because Page Farm is actually a magazine style site you're going to have to go through a few more steps to set up your site. The good thing is they have plenty of video tutorials to get you up and running.

The first thing you're going to have to do is set up an issue number. The easiest way is to set it up yearly. You can go monthly, or quarterly, but it will mean more work keeping things up to date.

Next you set up sections. If you take a look at Q C Jobs For You, we set up separate sections for Search Jobs, Interviewing, Resumes, Cover Letters, and the like. If you are going to offer advertisers a Featured Job section, I would place it at the top of your second column.

Right now, we have the large banner at the top set up with the logo of the HR guy at his desk, but as I start transitioning over to paid local advertising, that will become our prime advertising space. My thought is I can rotate five to seven ads through there at $350.00 per month, or more.

The banner and setting boxes will be helpful when you start posting advertising. You can experiment with using them to post content or infographics as you are getting started.

Monetizing your site

Ok, you've got a working site. The next challenge is getting it to make money.

Your main money maker is going to be your job board. Both, Indeed and Simply Hired, pay you every time someone clicks on a sponsored ad. The payout is made quarterly, if you meet minimum thresholds to receive a payment. Simply Hired pays out at $500. Indeed pays out at $100.

How much money you actually make, depends upon how much traffic you can drive to your site, and how many ads they click on. Getting started, my checks averaged $150.00 to $200.00 a quarter. After I started ramping up traffic, most of my checks were for $1000.00 to $1200.00.

Both sites pay you a commission for each advertiser who posts a listing with them. I charge $149.00 per listing. Indeed charges me a flat $20.00 per job posting, leaving me a profit of $129.00. Simply Hired splits the earnings 50/50 with you. That means I would receive $74.50 for each ad placed.

I don't know about you, but I'd rather have $129.00 profit, which is the major reason I use Indeed to power my job boards.

Another source of income when you are starting out is Google AdSense.

AdSense is it lets you look like a big player, no matter how small you are. It shows lots of ads from large national companies, along with ads from local businesses. AdSense pays out monthly, as long as you meet a $100 minimum threshold.

Getting started it will probably take three months before you see your first check. As traffic starts to build AdSense payouts should be pretty regular.

Similar advertising programs are available from Chitka.

Amazon offers an affiliate program that will pay you from four to eight percent of the selling price for customers you refer to their site. They also offer a great selection of banner ads and widgets you can use to target traffic. What I like about their program is you can target specific items. Say you decide to review a book; you can add an affiliate link to it and get paid for each copy sold.

Another program a lot of websites use is ClickBank. ClickBank lets you include a hop link to products from their site. They pay you a commission for each person you refer that purchases a product there. Many payouts range from $10.00 to $30.00 per sale.

Link Share is another program that I've had some success with. Like ClickBank, they only pay you when someone you refer either buys something, or submits a lead, depending upon the program requirements. The one problem with Link Share is many of the advertisers want to personally approve you before they let you get started. If you are just starting out, have low traffic, or don't meet their standards, many of them won't approve you for their program. As a result, you're not eligible for the best paying affiliate programs.

Selling local advertising

Selling local advertising will be your most profitable option. However, I wouldn't suggest trying it for at least six months to a year. Let your traffic and reputation build before start approaching local advertisers.

Local advertisers are going to require proof of traffic to your site. To do this you will need to engage an analytic program such as Google Analytics. It tracks visitors to your site, to individual pages, and it will tell you which sites referred visitors to you, and how long each visitor spent on your site.

Don't approach local advertisers until you can show them all of this information and a steady stream of traffic to your site.

Driving traffic to your site

Building your site will be easy. Driving traffic to it is a whole different animal.

There's a lot of talk on the web about SEO, and all sorts of tricks you can play to rank high in Google search. That's pretty much all it is – TALK!

There are two basic ways to drive traffic to your website:

1) You can post quality original content on a regular schedule and wait for search engines to find you.

2) You can pay for traffic.

The fact is you will probably want to do a little bit of both.

Google, Yahoo, and Bing all offer search ads that will funnel traffic to your site. Clicks (visitors) are sold to the highest bidder, and can bring a flood of traffic to your website, depending upon how much you're willing to spend. Depending on your market, and how many sites are bidding on similar keywords, visitors can cost you anywhere between 5 cents and fifty cents per click. I've always limited my bid to about thirteen cents, with an average cost of nine cents per click. That means for every $100.00 I spend on advertising, I received approximately 1100 visitors.

The best way to get a steady stream of traffic to your website is to post great content. To do this you need to post at least two articles per week, and tie them in with local cities and businesses. The articles don't have to be long. They can be as short as 250 to 350 words. They need to focus on providing local content.

The way I do it, is to write two short articles each week, and one longer article of 1000 to 2500 words.

Most readers are just going to skim through your content, so use plenty of headings. Include a lot of great pictures. Include pictures of people, businesses, and products. The more varied your content, the better your chances of being picked up in search.

Final words of advice

No matter what your subject, a website isn't going to make you money fast. Sometimes it happens in six months, sometimes a year, sometimes several years, and sometimes it won't come together no matter how hard you try. That's the way it works.

The best advice I can give you is keep plugging away at it. Post quality content to your site regularly. Buy PPC advertising when you can afford it, and tell everyone you come across about your site.

I've put up banners, passed out tote bags, pens, t-shirts, mugs. You name it, I've tried it. Make <u>Vista Print</u> your friend, and put whatever profits you can back into promoting your website.

The money will follow.

Have you ever thought life would be so much easier if there was: Someone there to help you through the rough spots? Someone you could bounce your ideas off of? Someone who could help you tame the ideas running wild in your head?

That's exactly what a coach does. She's the one who listens to what you have to say. She asks you questions to help you clarify your goals, and then she works with you to develop a plan that helps you move from point A to Point B.

And, most often, she does it all through a series of internet coaching sessions.

Other coaches offer internet training classes to help people develop all sorts of skills including,

1) Training people to how sell on eBay

2) Teaching people how to manage small business finances with QuickBooks

3) Helping people develop a personalized weight loss program

4) Showing people how to plan for a career change, get ready for retirement, and how to sell their house in today's down market

You name it, and somebody's probably running an online training class to help people solve their problems.

This section will show you how to get started with this great career opportunity.

Getting Started

Getting started in online coaching is often as easy as hanging your shingle out, and screaming here I am – Expert for hire!

The great thing about the coaching business is: No licenses or certifications are required to get started. The bad thing about the coaching business is: No licenses or certifications are required to get started.

Do you see the Catch 22?

There are no legal or training barriers to getting started, but you're going to be out there in a business environment surrounded by a lot of quacks and charlatans.

So how do you stand out from the crowd?

1) You need to be a real expert in the field you choose to become a coach in. You need to know what you're talking about. That means you need to walk the walk, and talk the talk of the people you are coaching.

2) While it's not required, a Bachelors degree, or advanced degree in the field you want to coach in will add credibility.

3) A certificate in coaching can help, if it is from a good training program.

4) You need to keep up with the latest coaching methods and delivery systems.

Going back to point number one, the best coaches are the ones who've been working in a particular field for their entire life. They have the practical experience people that can really help people.

If you don't have the practical experience, the next best thing is academic training. If you have an MBA in online marketing, you have the knowledge people need to build their web based businesses.

A quick Google search will return plenty of online certification programs promising to make you a coach. Many of them offer great training that will give you a head start at launching your online coaching business. Others are certificate mills, designed to make money, rather than show you how to get started. Be sure to perform your own *due diligence* before enrolling in any program.

Online coaching is a business. To be successful you need to understand how other successful coaches are conducting their business. You need to keep up with the latest internet technologies, such as Skype and GoToMeeting.

What does a coach do?

Before you get started you need to know what a coach does.

Many people think a coach is like a teacher. They are actually more like a mentor.

Here's the difference: A teacher spoon feeds you knowledge, and tells you how to do something. A coach helps you clarify your goals, and create an action plan for moving from Point A to Point B. Once the action plan is decided upon, the coach is responsible for making sure their client acts upon it.

Listening is one of the most important skills you are going to need. Your job is to get your client talking, and help them to see themselves more clearly. To do this, you ask questions and challenge them to expand on their ideas.

The biggest thing you need to do is get people thinking about where they are, and what it's going to take to get them where they want to be.

If you're a career coach and your client is looking to make a career change, you need to help them look at the whole picture. That means helping them see where they are today. You need to help them look at what skills they need to be successful in a new career. After that, you help them identify what skills they currently have, what skills they need to develop, and if they need to add any training or certification programs to get there.

The final step is to help your client develop an action plan for achieving their goal. You need to help them layout the steps, and hold them accountable for moving from Point A to Point B.

Couldn't your client do the same thing for themselves?

Your clients could do the same thing themselves, but think about yourself, or some of the people you know.

It's easy to say so and so should have done... But, when it comes to yourself, it's often harder to make a decision. Sometimes we're too hard on ourselves; sometimes we're too easy on ourselves. It's hard to see the big picture when you're talking about yourself. That's why so many people are turning to coaches. They need help to make important changes in their life. More importantly, they need someone to make them accountable for making those changes.

Online training

Online training is similar to coaching, except you are delivering a compact solution to your student's problems.

Most online training classes are tightly focused. They teach one skill. Examples are:

- How to use QuickBooks in your small construction business
- How to sell collectibles on eBay
- Selling on eBay for seniors
- Wedding cake decorating
- How to start a window washing business

Notice how focused each of the classes is. People want to learn specific skills that will help them solve a problem TODAY.

Your class can help them make money. You could focus your class on helping new mothers slim down after having a baby. Other classes teach kids how to care for their aging parents who've moved into their homes.

You name a topic, and there are going to be thousands of people interested in learning about it.

I've got an idea, how do I deliver it

Often times getting an idea for a training class is easy, figuring out how to deliver it can be the challenge.

Keep in mind, everyone learns in a different way, and at a different pace.

Some people are visual.

They need to see something to be able to do it. To teach these people, you're going to need to train them in person, or deliver their training through a series of videos.

Other people learn by reading.

This group would benefit from an online course where most of the information is delivered in text and charts. In this situation you would deliver the information through an online platform, or a series of weekly emails. During the class you could give assignments and quizzes to keep the class interactive. You would also need to make time to follow up with students by email or phone if necessary.

Webinars are great way to deliver online training.

GoToMeeting offers some great software for conducting online training sessions. I have attended many seminars delivered on their platform. Most last from forty-five minutes to an hour and a half.

You can let students watch you talk; you can use a whiteboard system; or you can show Power Point slides to enhance your talk. The program also lets presenters provide PDF's of the presentation that attendees can print to follow along, or keep for future reference.

Putting it all together

Online training classes are a great solution for delivering focused training to your clients.

To get started, you need to decide upon the method of delivery you are going to use. Earlier we talked about: Using an online teaching platform, email courses, and webinars.

After you have decided on a delivery method for your training class, you need to develop your material.

Most online training classes run from four to six weeks. They last approximately forty-five minutes to an hour per session. You want to keep them short and focused.

You need to tailor your presentation to the subject you are teaching. If you're conducting an online review for bankruptcy lawyers, your material is going to be at a higher level, than a class presented to teenage mom's on how to breastfeed their new babies.

Most trainers teach at the eighth grade level. That way they know most of their students will understand the material they are presenting.

You also want to think about your own style. If you are photogenic, and enjoy being out in front of people, you may want to conduct in person seminars, and then sell videos of them, as your online training class.

This is becoming more and more popular as the price of in person seminars goes up.

One person who does this is Lynn Dralle, who bills herself as the Queen of Auctions. She has written several books on eBay auctions, and conducts live training sessions as well. She recorded her 2008 Boot Camp on eBay selling and is offering it as Boot Camp in a Box for $997 a pop.

Think about it. You teach a weekend seminar once, at $2500 or more a head; you record it; and sell it for years at a thousand dollars a crack.

What could be better than that?

What about training books?

We already talked about Kindle books.

What if you create a series of short training books, and sell them from your own website? Charging $39.00 to $249.00 each, depending upon the information you have in them.

In this case your $2.99 Kindle book could be the bait to take people to your more focused, and expensive training classes.

To do this properly, you need a website. You also need to build an authority platform around yourself, and your products. One Kindle author who is doing a great job of this is Steve Scott.

Steve has an authority website he encourages all of his Kindle readers to visit for a free eBook. After he has you on his email list, he gets back to you every few weeks with info on his new books as they are released, or about any sales he is offering. You can visit Steve at <u>Steve Scott site</u> to see what he is doing.

Final wrap up

Think outside of the box!

Determine what you are good at. Create a niche where you become the expert in it. Write books. Create short reports. Make videos, and audio tapes of you presenting your material.

Most importantly build a website or blog that can act as a home base for all of your consulting and training activities.

Remember, all good things take time. Grow your business slowly. Add activities that enhance your business, and grow your authority in your niche.

If you plan to do several distinct things, create a separate identity, and website for each activity.

Doing too many things will confuse your audience, and cost you sales.

Good luck and great success in your new business.

Remember every success starts, by taking the first step. After that, a series of baby steps will move you along your path.

Thank you for purchasing this book. **Sell It Online 2** is an attempt to bring you easy to implement solutions for starting your online business. While no book can guarantee you success, the author and publisher have made every attempt to bring you the latest information that has been found to work for other online sellers. As with anything else in life results can vary, based on the time you invest and your approach to implementing the various ideas and strategies given.

If you find the contents helpful, please consider taking a few moments to leave a review on Amazon.

Your comments will help other readers decide if this book may be useful to them as they search for more information about how to sell online. They will also help me to catch errors or omissions in this book, and to correct them as quickly as possible.

If you really like what you read, and are feeling a little extra love, help me get the message out there. Tweet and share this book with all of your friends on Facebook. If you know someone who is dreaming about starting a career in online sales, gift them a copy or two.

www.ingramcontent.com/pod-product-compliance
Lightning Source LLC
Chambersburg PA
CBHW051222170526
45166CB00005B/2005